Tornado of Thoughts

AF624734

Vidushi

BookLeaf Publishing
India | USA | UK

Presentation by *BookLeaf Publishing*

Web: www.bookleafpub.com

E-mail: info@bookleafpub.com

ISBN: 9789363303324

First edition 2024

Dedicated to all those who have always screamed in silence.

ACKNOWLEDGEMENT

This book is a reflection of a journey, one that has been shaped by the love, support and wisdom of many.

I would like to thank–

My Mother, who always encouraged me and taught me the power of kindness and the strength of a compassionate heart.

My Father, who always supports me and whose life lessons have shaped my understanding of the world.

Life lessons, that life has offered me both the joyous and the challenging, shaped me into the person I am today. It is through these moments of reflection and growth that I have come to explore the depths of my inner self.

BookLeaf Publishing, for their trust in my work and for providing the platform to bring this book to life. Your professionalism and dedication have made this process smooth and fulfilling.

Lastly, to every reader who has picked up this book, thank you for sharing in this exploration of the human spirit. May these pages resonate with you and inspire your journey of self-discovery and healing.

PREFACE

'Sometimes to just breathe feels like a win'.

Writing these poems has been a journey, a journey through the corridors of my soul and a mirror held up to the souls of others. In moments of loneliness, I found words that comforted me like an old friend.

In heartbreak, I uncovered verses that gave voice to my pain. It is for those who have felt the weight of the world on their shoulders and for those who have discovered the strength to stand tall despite it all. It is for anyone who has ever felt broken and for everyone on the path to becoming whole again.

A gentle reminder that within every wound lies the potential for healing. This story is as much yours as it is mine. As you read these verses, may you find the courage to embrace your emotions, the strength to rise above your struggles and the peace that comes with knowing you are not alone on this journey.

Sending Love and Strength.

CONTENTS

Hidden Chapters

"I tried every possible way
to forget my pain
but turning everything into poetry
healed a part of me."
– writing heals

there are some chapters
in our lives
that we refused to
read in the light,
those chapters belong to the dark
filled with pain and scars,
we are struggling to be brave
so we keep those chapters in the grave.

Exhaustion

"Every time they silenced you
to gulp down your words,
and you started believing that
speaking up is a crime."

– when silence choked you

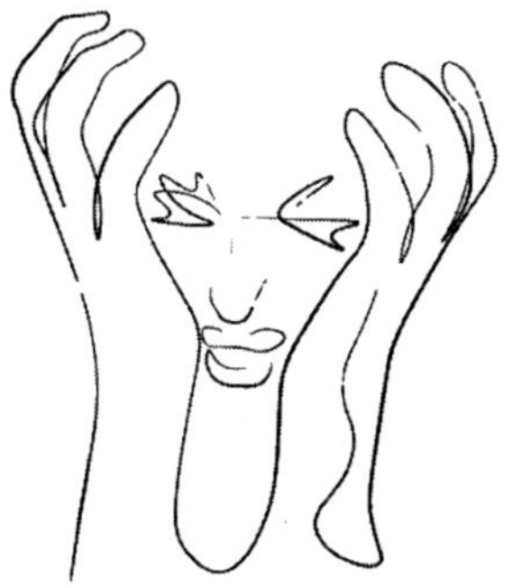

sometimes, i want to write
but my hands won't stop shaking,
sometimes, i want to sleep
but my mind won't stop thinking,
sometimes, i want to breathe
but my heart won't stop racing,
sometimes, i want to die
but my dreams won't let me.

Lost Me

"The raging thoughts of my mind
are making me lose my precious time,
I'm drowning deep
in the thoughts of grief."
– losing mind

it feels like
i’m losing my mind
even being so kind,

it feels like
i’m suffocating
it's so hard to breathe,

it feels like
i’m always stressed
possessed with loneliness,

it feels like
to die sometimes
but there is no choice,

it feels like
i’m sad every time
with a big smile.

Scars

"Scars have the deepest secrets."
– untold stories

maybe,
the acne on my face

is like a graveyard
that shows what is dead inside,

is the buried dream
that i've been carrying for a long time,

is the buried hope
because of the fear and low confidence,

is the buried betrayal
that i've failed to overcome,

is the buried feeling
that prevent me from falling in love again,

they all became part of my life
sticking always to my face,

and reminding me
all the buried things i have inside.

Darkness

"Darkness is my friend
that is always beside me,
defending me from demons
and giving me peace."
– when darkness is your companion

they asked me
why i like darkness so much,
i feel like i'm glowing
even if i'm living in darkness
i like dark rooms
i can stay there for hours,
i like night
it gives me peace
it doesn't mean i don't like lights
it's just that i feel
more comfortable in the darkness,
because in nights
it's just you
your tears
your dreams
your sadness
your smile
nobody can see you
you find 'you'
when you listen to yourself.

Tired Heart

"Your demons scared you
but you got so comfortable with them
that letting them go hurts you."
– when they become your friends

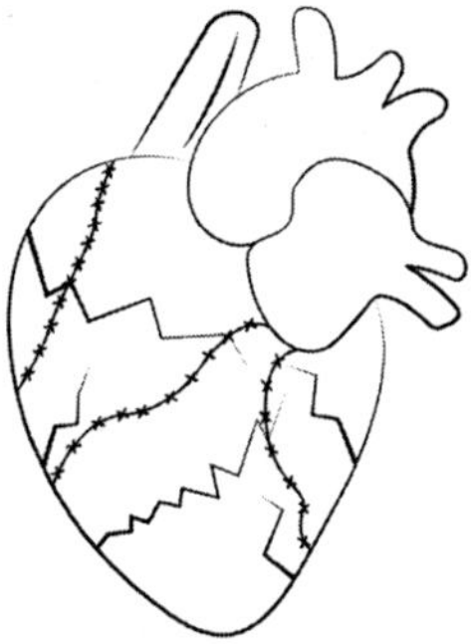

some flowers refuse to bloom
in someone's heart
because they once gave their flowers
to those they loved,

but they were treated
as if they had a cold heart
so it became a barren land
where light hasn't reached for years.

Stay Away From Negativity

"They keep telling you
about your flaws
that aren't even flaws,
you should keep
ignoring them
and be confident in yourself."
– focus on your work

walking is good for your health
so remember to walk away from toxic people
too,
because
cutting those connections
allows you to detach from suffocation
and breathe the air you deserve.

We Feel Too Much

"Sometimes you feel too much
that you can't explain,
but your heart is strong enough
to absorb any kind of pain."
– you have strength, more than you think

sometimes our tears
won’t validate our sadness
we are told by them
to stop crying over silly things,

they denied the fact
that we feel too much
and we end up in the war
with ourselves.

Dead Soul

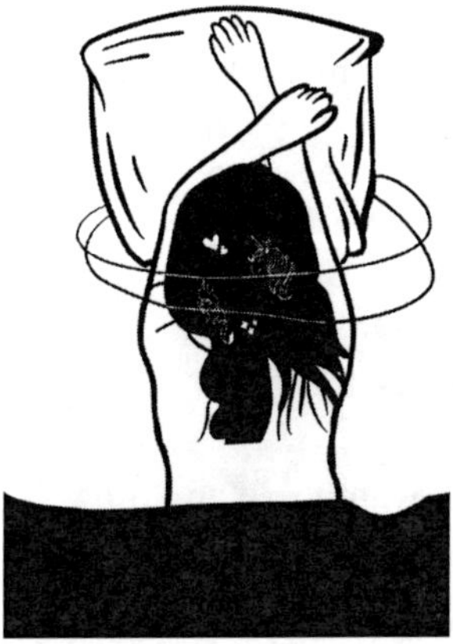

"There are a lot of invisible scars
in my heart,
it bleeds on paper
whenever it hurts."
– when you are surrounded by darkness

when your soul is tired
for so long
your body stops responding
as it did before
you are awake
but fail to get out of the bed,

you are dying
but forced to smile
your body needs food
but you don't want to eat
you are not lazy
but you don't want to do anything,

it feels like
something is stopping you
from doing the things you want
you try to move forward
but something is pulling you backward
you are living
but not enjoying,

you want to fulfil your dreams
but you have no motivation
you always try to motivate yourself
but always end up hurting yourself
still, you are trying, failing, learning and
growing
to give peace to the inner self.

Lowest Point

"When nothing
makes you feel alive."
– hopeless

once, i was good at everything
look at me now, good at nothing,
once, people considered me as an inspiration
look at me now, they call me dumb,
once, i cried a lot because i lost my dear ones
look at me now, i don't care if anyone wants to leave,
once, i wanted everyone to be with me
look at me now, i don't want anyone,
once, i enjoyed everyone's company
look at me now, i love to be alone,
once, i cared for places and people so much
look at me now, if they don't care, i ignore them,
once, i loved him madly
look at me now, i'm not able to fall in love again,
once, i was a fast learner and always wanted to learn something
look at me now, i can't do anything, even if i want to,
once, i always remembered god
look at me now, it feels like something is pulling me away from him,
once i cared for myself, at least basic things
look at me now, i don't know what i'm trying to do,
once, i was a happy kid

look at me now, i have become a lost, lonely and hopeless soul,
once, i dreamed of so many things to fulfil in my life
look at me now, i haven't even finished one dream yet,
once, i loved myself with all my scars
look at me now, i’m not able to love myself,
once, i was good at most things
look at me now, good at nothing.

Only Child

"People told me
that you are lucky,
I believe feeling alive
is the luckiest thing."
– don't forget your blessings

they told
those who are only children
are the lucky ones
no,
some chapters don’t exist for us
we don't have siblings who love and fight,
we don’t have permanent friends
who hide us from our parents
for making silly mistakes,
we feel lonely at home
as we don’t have anyone to talk to
yes, i agree,
we don't have to share
our room, food, toys or anything
but deep inside
we wish for someone
with whom we can share,
when we are sad, ill or feeling low
these materialistic things won’t help
but if we had a sibling
they would definitely do something to make us
smile
we miss these nonexistent chapters of our lives.

Childishness

"When you are not loved properly
when you are not understood properly,
while growing up
you end up searching for love
at all the wrong places."
– when you are not healed

never stop a child
from expressing childish behaviour
the more you try to stop them
the more they will bury their childishness
and become silent,

in adulthood
they seek someone
to whom they can open their childishness and
end up getting betrayed
because they became too innocent
in this cruel world.

Black

"I like all shades of black
even if darkness suffocates me."
– when darkness comforts you

as a child
i wished for the ghost to be my friend,
later, i realised
how broken that child was
to trust any humankind.

Burning Environment

"Those who burned in a home
find it difficult to find a home."
– when home doesn't give you peace

when you had grown up
in the burning environment
where you were confused
between anger and kindness,

in adulthood, you end up choosing
the people who burn you
because they remind
the environment
of your childhood.

Pain

"You always try to find love
where you have been lost
and then
you feel lost again."

– some mistakes happen even if
we don't want to

the child who has suffered
enough pain since childhood
finds it difficult to share that pain,
and starts believing
that pain is the only thing
that makes us feel alive.

Heavy Heart

"You feel empty
but your heart is still heavy."
– when you have so much to say

when you begged at home
to be understood
you end up with someone
who failed to understand you,

sometimes it feels like
heartbreak sounds like a thunderstorm
and the heavy rains
shows how much pain the heart is carrying.

Hurting

"Maybe my writing looks normal
but it's the scream I have been carrying for a long time."

– trust me, silence is heavy

i don’t want to die
but i feel like
i don’t want to live either,
as broken pieces
hurts me a lot.

To Feel Home In A Home

"Trying to be normal
but forgot
it's impossible
without pain."
– when pain is the only memory left

those who were left alone
in childhood
find it difficult
to attach to someone,

when people say
'i want to go home to feel like home'
but why is it difficult for some people
to feel like home in a home?

Unhealed Trauma

"I am alive
but the graveyard is inside me."
– unsaid stories

you know
why sometimes you find peace
in stormy winds
at least they can understand
your mental state,

you know
sometimes you cry
without any reason
because
the child in you
never cried at the times
when it has to.

Understand Them

"Be happy with what you have."
– Gratitude

sometimes you wonder
why your parents fail to understand you
maybe they also carry
some unhealed traumas
that shapes their behaviour
in a certain way,

sometimes when you think deeper
you realise everyone is trying
to cope with their traumas
in their own way.

Maa

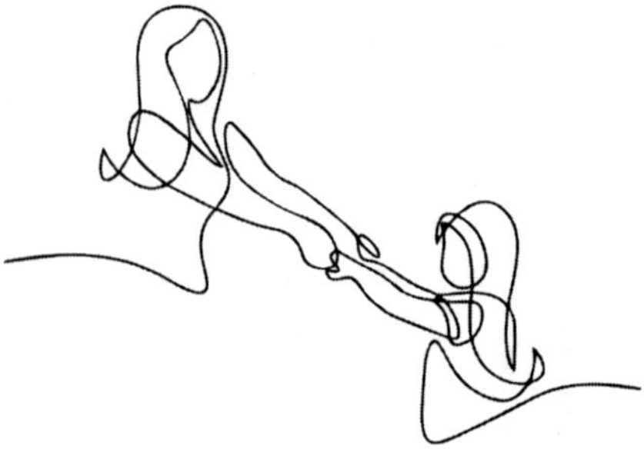

"She will support you
when nobody else does."
– purest soul

when everything around feels dark
when confusion clouds my path
when i feel demotivated as hell
when everyone says i'll fail
then only the presence of my maa brings light
so i can choose the path that feels right
my confidence level soars to new heights
and i prove to everyone that i can achieve
anything in my life
because my maa is always by my side,

when i feel alone and low
when i need someone to talk to
when i feel emotionally hurt
when i feel a lot of pain
when i'm not well
then my maa becomes my best friend
she refreshes my mood within a second
she has a big golden heart
that takes care of every little thing on earth,

even if my maa has a bad day
even if my maa is not well
even if my maa is tired
even if my maa works at home and office
the whole day and night
still, she manages everything so right
nobody will ever take the place of my maa

because she gives everything at any cost
just to make me smile.

Super Hero

"He may be rough around the edges,
but his heart is pure and invaluable."
– father

he fulfilled wishes
even before we ask
he cares for the family
without saying a single word,

he also feels sad and gets upset
but never shows he is distressed
his anger seems dangerous
maybe because he hides his emotions,

he is the protector of the family
we should respect him wholeheartedly
in every storm, in the darkest times
he loves, he cares and he fights day and night,

whatever the situation is
he is the backbone of the family
and we always wish
that his laughter is always filled with joy.

Heal First

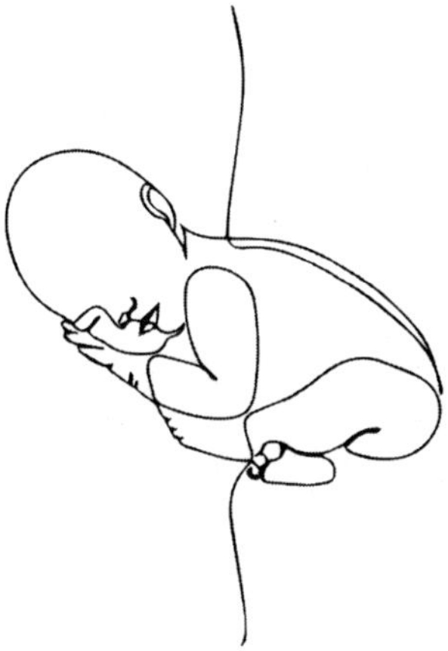

"The absence of love in the home
makes you seek love
where everyone fails to provide."
– when you end up seeking love
in the wrong places

i hope
everyone makes children
only when they are healed
only when they have the courage
so that,
their children won't
carry the baggage
that makes them
underconfident
fearful
and hard to trust anybody.

Learning To Bloom

"The flower
that may bloom
in the future,
was plucked as a bud."
– childhood traumas

new places
new peoples
i was all alone
i missed my old places
i missed my old friends
i cried
i screamed
no one heard
i became silent
avoiding violence,

they bullied me
i ignored them
they hurt me
i forgave them
they teased me
i remained silent
not because i didn't care
but because i didn't know
how to react to them,

i felt numb
earlier, i was dying
i needed
someone to talk to me
someone to stay with me
later, i became so silent.
that i even stopped listening to myself

i started liking to be alone
i started liking to stay in a room
i avoided meeting people
i could only feel fear
now avoiding anyone who comes near,

now i’ve grown up
struggling to overcome my fear
struggling to gain confidence
and i realised that
if they hadn't plucked me as a bud
i would have blossomed much earlier
however, i’m not losing hope
i’m watering my roots
making my dead soul alive
so that i can live the fullest
for the rest of my life.

Everyone Needs Someone

"All are part of our life
but not the whole life."
– bitter truth

in this vast world
we need a hand
the one who holds us till the death
the one who always supports us
the one who always motivates us
the one who always cares for us
the one who always loves unconditionally
the one who behaves like a friend,

that 'one' can be our mother or father,
brother or sister, bf or gf, friends, children
or any other relationship
but the reality is
that 'one' hand
is not always available to us,

everyone plays a part in our life
there is a contribution from all the people
who are connected with our life
so stay positive
even if you are feeling alone
believe in yourself
you can achieve anything in your life.

Natural Therapy

"Whenever you feel lonely
spend time with nature."
– healer

the sunrise
and the sunset,
the cloudy sky
and a garden filled with butterflies,
the rainfall
and the mountains with waterfall,
the running water of the lake
and the fight between the mongoose and the
snake,
climbing upon the trees
and watching fish in the sea,
playing with kids
without using cell phones instead,
helping the needy
without being greedy,
sometimes stay alone
and it feels like you are in a comfort zone,
all these things can give you peace
just feel them deep,
because sometimes
these are better than taking a long sleep.

Listen To Your Inner Voice

"Your inner self
always tries to
give you a message,
never ignore that."
– inner voice

there is a yelp
in the late-night
have you ever heard that?

not in the surroundings
not from someone else
it's within ourselves, deep inside
have you ever heard that?

a part that is
screaming inside
crying inside
dying inside
and it's
hidden from all
have you ever heard that?

someone who
boosts you inside
makes you strong inside
recover your wound inside
makes you happy inside
it's only your inner voice
have you ever heard that?

Power Of Listening

"To say something is nice
to listen to someone is an art."
– listening is an art

i never understood
the power of listening
until i became silent
when nobody listens to me
i keep silent in every situation
because
i don't understand
how to express myself,

so i started listening to people
i became good at listening
but i still fail to express
the part of me that was hurt in childhood
i haven't recovered yet
the child in me still wants
someone to listen
someone to understand
but i’ve no energy
to express myself,

i think that's how
i turned into a writer
i write
when nobody listens
and it doesn't affect me now
if nobody hears me,

still, there is a craving to be heard
but i don't know when
the child in me will heal
till then, i’ll write with all my heart
to cope with pain and heal my scars.

Doubting Yourself

"Slowly turning into the person
I never wanted to be."

– fails to recognise myself

when you are at your lowest
you think
you don’t deserve to be loved,
when loneliness hits its peak
you feel like
you are the dumbest creature on earth,
when you want to do many things
yet end up doing nothing.

Changed Me

"Incidents will change you."
– a new version of you

now, the silence you see in me
once it was an unstoppable utter,
now, the hesitation you see in me
once it was only frankness,
now, i prefer to be alone
once it was all about socialising,
now, you see a less talkative me
once it was only craziness residing in me,
now, i am frank with the close ones
once it was with anyone,
now, i am thinking more practically
once it was all about emotions,
now, i have less time for myself
once it was all about others,
now, i'm busy
focusing on improving myself,
some people have become part of my life
and some have departed,
but,
time changes
people change
moment changes
so do i,
and in the end
only the 'self' remains.

Silence

"Silence
is never empty,
it has the
weight of words."
– silence says a lot

some incidents of my life
changed me completely
i always felt alone
in my room
in a crowd
in my thoughts
everywhere,

sometimes
every single thing around me
made me realise that
i’m alone
because
i’m an only child,

i always stayed alone in the house
when my parents worked in different states
when i felt like the odd one out among friends
i thought maybe god was giving me signs
you have to be alone to live this life,

suddenly, a guy came into my life
it feels like i’m not alone anymore
and when he left
it felt like ending myself
i was not able to cope
with my feelings
and i felt more alone
than before,

now, i’m afraid to attach
with anyone else in my life
i’m keeping distance from everyone
so that i won’t get attached to anyone
and can cope with my existing pain.

Isolation

"Sometimes
I wanna disappear
to validate my intuition
that nobody cares."
– strangely it's true

isolation
becomes your daily routine
escaping from people
helps you in living,
overthinking thoughts
become your friend
even if you want to
you're not able to unfriend them,

how strange it is
living alone gives you peace
at the cost of your mental health
your mind tells you
that you will heal alone
until you realise
it's breaking you inside,

and you want someone
to talk with you
but whom to talk to
still, you don't know
so isolation
keeps you away
from the reality of the world
and you are comforting yourself
in your imaginary world.

Want To Hug Myself

"When you start loving your scars,
you are not afraid of more scars."
– when you are on your healing journey

sometimes i wish
to go back to my childhood
and hug my younger self,
to tell her
you have to let go of certain things,
you have to learn this on your own
you have to trust yourself
and one day
everything will be fine.

Men In Love

"My day is incomplete
without talking to you,
no scenery is beautiful
without you."

– true love

the guy who never fell in love
started falling in love with her,
the guy who never read a novel
started reading it,
the guy who never cared for himself
started caring for her,
the guy who never danced
started dancing with her,
the guy who never shared anything with anyone
started sharing the smallest details with her,
the guy who never hugged someone
started hugging her every day,
the guy who likes to live alone
wanted to spend the rest of his life with her.

Love

"You are my favourite place
my heartbeat becomes calm
my mind finds peace
whenever i'm in your arms."
– you felt like home

when i realised
that i’m in love
his arms feel safe to me
he seems like the world to me,
i’m ok with any sacrifice
only to see his smile
i feel complete with him
i already dream
of a beautiful life with him.

If I Tell You

"I was already yours
will you be mine?"

– delulu

if i tell you the truth,
what's going on in my mind
will you stay by my side?

if i tell you how much you mean to me,
what's going on in my heart
will you adore me?

if i tell you how i fell for you,
how fast my heartbeat races
will you hug me?

if i tell you that you complete me,
no matter the situation is
will you care for me?

if i tell you that you are the best thing that has
happened to me,
in every aspect of my life
will you believe me?

if i tell you i want to spend my life with you,
through every ups and downs
will you marry me?

Eyes Hold The Story

"My inner self talks to me in a poetic way."

– every time it heals a part of me

your eyes carry the charm
that the person who saw in them, may feel alive,
your eyes have depth
that for readers, it becomes their favourite place,
your eyes are like oceans
even non-swimmers want to dive in them,
your eyes hold the universe
every star twinkles in them,
your eyes are so mesmerising
that whoever sees, may fall in love with them,
your eyes have a spark
a dead soul will feel alive, just by looking into
them,
your eyes hold a story
after seeing, everything else stops in them.

To Be With You

"Broken in love
but still believe in love."
– lover of love

i wish i could touch you
the way i imagined
like,
holding hands
feeding you foods
patting your head
hugging you
just to feel you
in my arms
to be with you forever.

Failed To Express

"No one understands
wish I could hug myself."
– sometimes pat yourself

you know we failed terribly
to express ourselves
to our loved ones,
we were afraid that
they would stop loving us,

and
we tried to seek peace
with those
who gave us tragedies.

He

*"His eyes are so mesmerising
anyone can get lost in them."*
– just a delulu world

watching him
is my favourite thing,
he is calm as the moon
shines like a star,
he is as soothing as a breeze
healing my scars,
he hugs me like the wind
calming my overthinking,
i never imagined myself
without him,
he is like the missing piece
that can only fit in my heart.

Loving You

"You left me
and took away the keys to my heart,
now anyone who tries to enter
finds it locked."

– old memories

i loved you
like
the moon loves the sky
the sky loves the rainbow
the rainbow loves the rain
the rain loves the sand
the sand loves the tree
the tree loves the flower
the flower loves the bee
the bee loves the honey
the honey loved by you
the 'you' loved by me.

Begging Love

"Losing others is painful
but not as painful as losing yourself."
– don't let yourself down

we all have tried hard
to fit into someone's heart,
knowing that
we are not the piece of a puzzle
that fits with them,

we all begged for love
from someone
who wanted to run away,
until you realised
they never deserved a chance
to be chased.

He Pretended

"I had mistaken that
his eyes were full of love
later, I realised
I saw the reflection of my eyes in his eyes."
– when you love someone blindly

i loved him
in every possible way
i loved him
in every simplest way
staring at him
until his eyes met mine
listening to his voice
felt like paradise,

when he held my hands in his
it felt like we were destined
until i realised
these feelings were just from my side
he just pretended to be mine,

still, i had hope
that he would change
that's the mistake
i made
i should stop adoring him
i should stop begging for love from him
i should stop crying for him
i should stop thinking that he is mine,

i always considered him a part of me
when he left
he broke my heart
i'm left with the scars

i prefer to be alone
rather than being with someone
i'm broken
still, i've faith in love
because of the way i loved.

Unanswered Prayers

"When one prayed to be together forever
and the other prayed for a breakup."
– the universe always gives you a sign

i prayed for you
i prayed for us
but my prayers
went unanswered
maybe,
those unanswered prayers
are the actual answers
that we are not destined.

Broken

"If you have to remind them
to ask about your well-being,
they are not yours."
– never beg love

i never liked
being touched
until you hugged me,
i never cried
this much
until you left me.

Self Respect

"Begging for love
is disrespecting yourself."
– respect yourself

no matter
how long have you known someone
how long have you cared for someone,
if they are continuously disrespecting you
you don’t want to stay in touch with them.

Toxic Relationship

"You are too terrified
that you can't differentiate
between fear and love."
– let your fear go away

when you have more fear
than love
from your partner
it's not worth staying,

some relationships
fail to provide love
when that's the only thing
you are craving.

Unkind People

"Loving you is like falling into darkness
the more I fall
the less I recognise myself."
– don't be blind in love

every human being
is capable of love,
every human being
is capable of trust,
still,
some choose to be toxic
some choose to cheat.

Black Became Companion

"Screams have different colours
but why mine is always black."
– when you have lost all your hopes

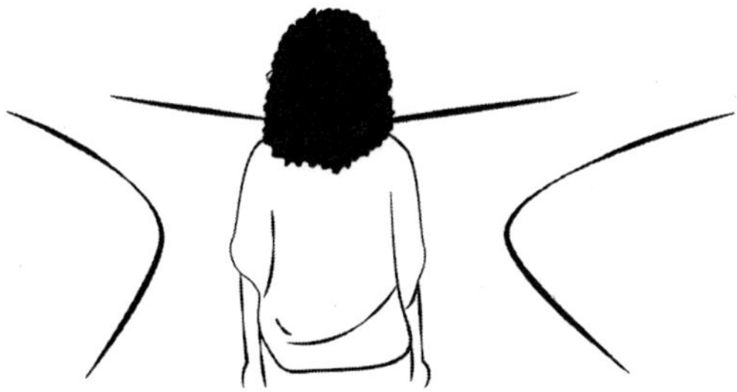

he added colours to my life
and took them all
while leaving,

i even lost all my existing colours
when he left me
black became my companion,

because
it hides my pain
it hides my tears
it hides my silent cries
it hides me from everyone
it hugs me
making me feel comfortable in the darkness.

I Still Starve For You

"Some memories
make a permanent place in our hearts."
– when memories play in a loop

i want to overcome my pain
but,
your memories pull me down
your eyes make me weak
your smile makes me feel alive
your pain makes me cry
your voice makes me fall in love again
your silence still i can listen,
i hope you understand
your care, which i still starve for
your support, which i still starve for
your unsaid love, which i still starve for.

Don't Be Blind

"You are addicted to being alone
when all you want is
someone to be with you."
– don't be with the wrong ones

you want someone
but you end up asking them
to put bandages on your scars,
still knowing that
they are the ones who have hurt you,

also,
they have given you an umbrella
while pushing you into the river.

Single Soul

"When everyone made you realise that you are better off alone."

– tired soul

maybe
i’m a single soul,
that’s why
i find myself alone everywhere
in surroundings
in gatherings
among people,

sometimes
i feel nice to be alone
but sometimes
it drains all my energy.

Feeling Strange

"When everyone enjoys their childhood
I'm dealing with my trauma
without knowing that
it is actually called trauma."
– some scars remain

mostly, i feel different among others
sometimes i wonder,
why am i not able to fit into this world?
why do i feel weird among them?
is there any problem with me?
am i the only one who feels like this?

Difficult Times

"You must be tired of being the shoulder
to your own shoulder."
– sometimes, let others help you

there are some difficult parts of us
that are hard to handle
even on days when we feel tired
we have to be strong
even if we are suffering too much
we still handle it gracefully,

sometimes
we want someone
to support us in those difficult times
to hold our hands
to hug us tight
little do they know
just this small gesture
can calm our racing mind.

Mixed Emotions

"It's been a long time
since I haven't met myself."
– missing self

some incidents leave us
in some weird way
we are sad
after a moment
we are laughing
then suddenly
we start crying,

experiencing mixed emotions
so frequently that
we fail to understand ourselves
we fail to analyse
what's going on in our lives,

we are trying our best
to cope with this mess
and in our darkest nights
we are trying to shine like a star
by accepting all our scars.

Demons

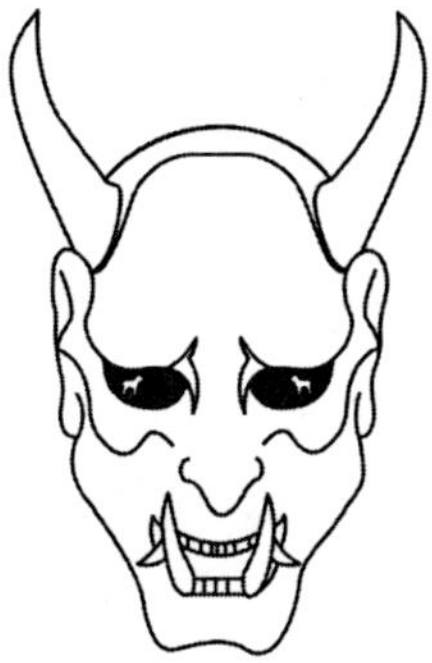

"Sometimes I feel so numb
that I fail to move."
– when the mind plays bad chapters of life

don’t you feel
that demons reside within us,
making us repeat mistakes
multiple times
and adding more baggage
to our healing journey.

Loner Wolf

"I am the light
of your dark nights."
– self to self

getting drowned
in my thoughts
deep down
everything haunts
feels like
lost in a black hole
i do not see
any ray of hope
crawling, walking, falling
to get out of here,
everywhere it's dark
and nobody cares,

crying, screaming
asking for help
they are making fun
and blame as an act
feeling lonely
and hopeless
started believing
i've to live in this mess
i've drowned so deep
it's hard to breathe,

i started hearing my inner voice
following its guidelines
started learning to swim
to fulfil my dreams

learned a lesson
you have to help yourself
if nobody brings the light
you have to keep moving
until you see the light.

I Still Believe In Love

"Be the right one
before expecting the right one."
– hoping for the best

i have seen some people
who still believe in old-school love
loving one partner their whole life
is all they want,

i have seen some men
who are ready to do anything
for their woman,

i have seen some women
who are willing to sacrifice anything
for their man,

i have seen some old couples
who are living examples
that only one partner is truly enough,

i have seen some young couples
who always stand up for each other
and end up marrying together,

i have seen these people
who made me believe
that, while it's rare in this generation
but true love really exists.

Repeating Mistakes

"I wish
I can take away
all the pain
of the girl in front of me
but I was looking at the mirror."
– you need to help yourself

sometimes you keep choosing
to make the same mistakes
even when you don't want to,
and crying over it
becomes a habit
because you were never taught
how to deal with mistakes,
instead, it becomes the
only pain you have
as a friend
that consoles your inner pain,
rather knowing that
it’s like touching the wound
before it heals,
and results in
increasing your pain.

Run Away

"Just because you are lost in the darkness
doesn't mean you can't find the sun."
– trust yourself, you can create magic

sometimes we all want to run away
from everything
and to stay in the mountains
because our kind heart
has been misunderstood and is tired,

somedays you will regret
for not doing the things
that you wanted badly,

somedays you will look back
and realise
that you should have done it.

Rewrite Story

"Those who remember everything
find it difficult to forget the bad chapters."
– when memories trigger frequently

sometimes i want to
vanish myself
to escape this world
and disappear,

i want to rewrite my story
but the past haunts me
and my future terrifies me
as i see the present in my life.

Trust Youself

"Some people
died in their childhood,
crying in adulthood
makes them feel alive."
– when you are used to pain

moving on is like
always running from the past
and if you keep running
you miss the present also,

we are waiting for someone
to heal us
knowing that
we need to heal by ourselves.

Create Art

"Sometimes
I feel dead
poetry helps me
to make me feel alive."
– poetry rhymes according to your heart

some heartbreaks tend to
make us believe that
pains are easy to carry,

i hope you mend your broken heart
into a piece of art
where flowers start blooming
and you find your way to living.

You Can Blossom Too

"You can bloom like flowers
and spread your positivity."
– trust your roots

whenever i see the blossoming flowers
it gives me hope
that one day, you will blossom too,

whenever i gaze at the sky
it gives me hope
that one day, you will shine like the sun too,

whenever i smell the fragrance of the flowers
it gives me hope
that one day, you will spread your positivity too,

whenever i think about the spring
it gives me hope
that after the fall, you will rise again too,

so,
whenever you feel low,
due to any falls in your life
just remember that
you can blossom like the flowers too.

Surviving

"I was so unkind to myself
still, rather than being kind
I just want to run away from myself."
– when you feel suffocated within you

i don't know
how to help myself
when all i want
is to leave everything
and run away to a place
where nobody knows me,

i don't know
how to swim
still, i'm wondering
how i survived
these many years
when i was actually drowning.

Moving On

"When I was in love
I became colourblind,
that's why
I wasn't able to recognise
the red flags in you."

– sometimes you should avoid what your heart says

i was like a flower
soft and gentle
you plucked me apart
vanished my existence
from the core of your heart,

it hurts me a lot
felt like a gunshot
still, i forgave you
and wanted a restart,

again, you hurt me
now i need a kickstart
my heart is tied by a knot
and i'm trying
to breathe
by untying that knot.

Healing

"From saying I am always there for you
to being there for everyone except me,
he really meant it."
– never force someone to stay

i have spent hours upon hours
days upon days
months upon months
years upon years
thinking about you,
and wrote poetry
about you
about us
about your love and lies
about your trust and betrayal
with all my heart,
and when you left
i burned them
and wrote more verses
from those ashes
to heal my broken heart
that helped me to move on
so that my heart can rhyme again.

Finding Home

"It's difficult to find home
when you are already staying in a home."
– you are your home

we are trying hard
to find peace
in every possible way
in every place
but sometimes
home doesn't feel like home
home doesn't feel like home with people
home doesn't feel like home in a place
because you are not at peace with yourself
when you are at peace with yourself
home feels within you.

Peaceful Night

"Loneliness is my friend
it made me love the darkness more
that's why
I love being alone more
I love the night more
I love the moon more."
– when you feel like a child of the universe

the night sky gives me peace
feels like it's hugging me
wrapping me in the stars
putting my head on the moon
he listens to me till i feel light
so i believe
at least here, everything is alright.

Forgiveness

"Don't remain sad
if you are broken
this happened so that
you can create a masterpiece."
– you can do anything

i want you to forgive those
who made you feel less important
who made you believe that
you don't deserve to be loved,

you know
we are loved by someone
we are hated by someone
what truly matters
is that you should start loving yourself
and then you will see the magic
that the universe loves you,

you are important
as you are a part of the universe
and you will realise
that you deserve to be loved
i hope this makes you feel
worthy and important.

Warrior

"Sometimes to just breathe feels like a win."
– when anxiety hits you

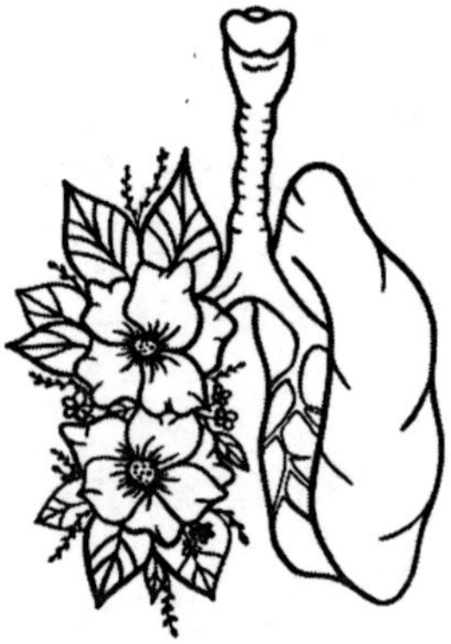

when a tornado of thoughts
is rushing in my mind
i’m not able to breathe
it feels like suffocating,

when i’m trying
to take a deep breath
and crying on the papers
to calm my inner self,

when people say to me
just calm down by holding my chin
how can i explain to them that
sometimes to just ‘breathe’
feels like a win.